ELEMENTS
OF
LEADERSHIP

J. L. CEARLEY

an imprint of The Reader's Digest Association, Inc.

LifeRich Publishing books may be ordered through booksellers or by contacting:

LifeRich Publishing
1663 Liberty Drive
Bloomington, IN 47403
www.liferichpublishing.com
1 (888) 238-8637

ISBN: 978-1-4897-0040-7 (sc)
ISBN: 978-1-4897-0041-4 (e)

Printed in the United States of America.

LifeRich Publishing rev. date: 11/12/2013

TABLE OF CONTENTS

Acknowledgements

No attempt to write a book is done in a vacuum. Over the period of writing this one, there have been many who encouraged me and supported my efforts to make this possible.

First and foremost, I want to thank the two women in my life who continue to give me a reason to want to help others— my mother Delrose and my wife Janett. Whenever I get discouraged, you are always there bolstering my spirit and giving me a reason to do more. My life has been blessed from birth by a woman who is the most spiritual person I know. In addition to her belief in God and in herself, she has always made me feel that I was special and capable of doing anything, as long as it was for good and was done right. She helped me to believe in myself from an early age. Then, the Lord blessed me with my darling wife, who always sees the best in me and supports me in a way that makes me not want to let her down. She is my soul mate and I cannot imagine life without her.

During the early days of the formulation of this leadership model, I was blessed with the friendship of Nelson dos Santos and Beverly Clarkson, two of my managers who listened to my mentoring from the underlying concepts of this book with anxious anticipation. By their attention and desire to learn more, they affirmed my belief this work could be beneficial to others.

Once the initial draft was completed, I had the good fortune to have several friends proofread it for grammatical errors. This help was beneficial, but their positive feedback and encouragement to proceed with publication was even more meaningful. For that, I need to acknowledge Quentin Baker, Doug Olson, Brooke Hildreth, Thane Cuevas, James Copeland, Lee Romain, and Steve Mack.

May God bless each of you for your contributions and for believing in me.

Introduction

One day in 2000, I was reflecting on almost 29 years of experience in the petrochemical industry, and I asked myself, "What had I learned working in two refineries and four chemical plants? What could I teach young supervisors and engineers that would keep them from repeating the mistakes of my past? What sense could I make of the countless revelations ("Ah, Ha!" moments) I had experienced and remembered?" After all, in addition to learning from my mistakes and observing the mistakes and successes of others, I had read countless books about management theory, gleaning bits and pieces from each. However, I was frustrated by the lack of a single leadership model that brought all of this together.

I soon realized that as much as we talk about it, leadership tends to remain an ambiguous commodity. And, we in industry tended to treat people as either possessing this rare commodity or not. We cherry picked those blessed with the inherent talents we desire and overlooked the rest. Seldom had I observed anyone attempting to teach leadership skills to people in their charge. I concluded that this had to stem from either our lack of understanding of what constitutes effective leadership or a belief that the skills could not be learned.

So, I began to list those elements of leadership that could be learned. The first list only contained seven elements, but at least it was a start. Over the next few years, the list grew to 13 elements; some were things to do and some were how to do them.

My next step was to use this list of elements as a model to teach these essential skills to people in my charge, those for whom I had the responsibility to develop. My initial attempt was not too successful. This was partly due to ineffective communication on my part and partly due to an unreceptive audience. However, with continued use I soon found that the list of elements could serve as an effective communication tool to provide other direct reports feedback on activities on a weekly basis. As my skill level increased with communicating these critical elements, they began to appreciate the counsel and actually encouraged me to provide more. Soon, I found that I was able to not only use the elements with direct reports, but also able to use them to guide members of other groups with whom I worked.

That was when I realized this list of critical elements might be the basis for a book. My goal was to write a relatively short book (no longer than 100 pages) to encourage easy reading. I also wanted it to be structured so that specific elements were easy to access for an easy refresher on an individual basis.

I don't pretend to have all the answers, but I do believe the following captures at least 80% of the necessary skills to be a good leader. I also want to note that much of this knowledge was gleaned from the countless books referenced herein. I don't believe any single book contains all the answers or all the knowledge on any subject, especially about Leadership or Management theory. And, the reason for writing this book is to make sense of a lifetime of learning; to put this knowledge into a useable form that will allow me to share the experiences with others; in short, to chronicle my journey. In the pursuit of knowledge, you will find elements that begin to weave a patchwork like a quilt that increases your understanding and makes you a better person. Take pride in your personal patchwork of knowledge.

Read and enjoy.

LEADERSHIP MODEL

The Leadership Model offered in these pages is actually a combination of "What to Do" and "How to Do It". Quite simply, Elements 1-5 are the "What to Do" portion and the remainder of the book is the "How to Do It" portion that helps to make it effective. For simplicity, the model will be presented in this manner:

<u>What to Do</u>

> Element 1—Personal Vision
> Element 2—Effective Communication
> Element 3—Be a Boundary Manager
> Element 4—Create Personal Empowerment
> Element 5—Make it Happen

<u>How to Do It</u>

> Element 6—Practice Lifetime Learning
> Element 7—Take the High Road
> Element 8—Think Synergistically
> Element 9—Make Heroes of Your People
> Element 10—Take Care of Personal Matters Expeditiously

Element 11—Share Your Passion

Element 12—Have Fun

Element 13—Remain Calm in Crisis

Conclusion—The Next Step

Each of these elements is presented as a separate lesson so you can refresh your memory as needed or concentrate on improvement opportunities.

The first two "What to Do" elements are the most critical for effective leadership. Developing a **Personal Vision** is the first step in elevating yourself to leadership status, and it forms the basis for everything else you do. The second element on **Effective Communication** is woven throughout the entire book because of its importance to every aspect of our lives. It emphasizes how effective communication begins with the understanding that every person with whom we interact has a desired amount of information they expect from us and there are consequences for not meeting that need.

"What to Do" Elements 3 and 4 about **Boundary Management** and **Creating Personal Empowerment** are two elements key to understanding your role as a leader or direct report (someone reporting to another in a supervisory relationship). Element 3 focuses on the role of the supervisor in creating space for individual creativity. Element 4 focuses on how a team member creates a level of autonomy within their created space. Effective use of these elements will fundamentally change your way of interacting with your team and increase the job satisfaction of your team.

"What to Do" Element 5, **Make it Happen**, focuses on your role as a leader in creating an action imperative. The best laid plans will seldom materialize unless you have the strength of character to initiate action and change the status quo.

The remaining eight "How to Do" elements provide you with required values, strategies, and supportive actions to help make the first five effective.

This is offered as a Leadership Model. It should actually be called a Leadership and Management Model because so much of it is applicable to good management, as well. Unfortunately, the word "management" has taken on such a stigma these days I hesitated to make it prominent for fear it might hit some "hot buttons", blinding readers to the truths herein before they have a chance to read and learn. "Management" is not bad. But, there are some bad managers. With the tools provided in these lessons, I believe any leader can improve their effectiveness and enhance their essential leadership skills.

PART I

WHAT TO DO

PERSONAL VISION

"Vision is not seeing things as they are,
but as they will be."—Unknown

Good leadership cannot exist without a **Personal Vision**. This should be intuitively obvious, because you simply cannot lead a group of people to a desired destination unless you know where you are going. And, more importantly, without a clear picture of where you want to go, it is impossible to articulate the picture in such a way that others will want to help you get there. Good leadership begins with a **Personal Vision**.

I hesitate to use the term "vision" because it is used indiscriminately and has become a part of "buzzword bingo" in industry. Mention this word and the eyes of many people will lose focus and become glazed. Since the 1980's, it has become fashionable to post a vision statement to communicate to the workforce and customers the desired state of the company. This is not bad. It does provide a common direction and an "end state" for all to achieve. In most cases, however, management selects a committee to draft a "Vision Statement" to help shape

ELEMENTS OF LEADERSHIP

the future of the company. This is done to obtain employee ownership. But, it is not a **Personal Vision** of leadership.

The vision I am talking about in this chapter and book is personal. It is your view of how your area of influence can be changed for the betterment of all concerned. It is the view of the future that you possess. This is the view of the future that you must communicate in detail to those who follow you. This is your view of the future that becomes so real and so desirable to your team they will want to help you attain it. This is the view of the future that will become so real they will want to develop their own view of the future that supports yours and helps them determine how to help you realize your vision.

People will follow a leader. They will naturally be drawn to someone who knows where they are going and can create a vision by communicating it in such a way it becomes a desirable place to be. In fact, people are hungry for visionary leadership. Unfortunately, vision is a commodity so rare that they will also follow a bad vision. How else can you explain an entire nation following the leadership of Adolph Hitler in Nazi Germany? The challenge for us is to develop a vision that provides a positive direction, with beneficial results.

Several years ago, I worked for Jimmie Bufkin, a man who came to our manufacturing site with a vision of transforming our work place into a site known for world class performance. His vision was still in the formative stages, and he was not sure how we were going to achieve it. But, he clung to his

2

vision and worked for a few years to make it real to us and to convince us that it was attainable. He had us read books on creating participative management in the workforce. He circulated articles about how others had transformed their workplace to utilize the full talents of the front line personnel, a place he hoped to take us. He spent time in management meetings discussing his vision and helped us to understand it. He shared his misgivings about failure and solicited our input about how to prepare for success. I am forever indebted to him for helping me understand the importance of a **Personal Vision** and its role in leadership. It took me some time to understand its impact.

One of the common misconceptions about vision is that it is like the visualization that is commonly used by athletes. Visualization techniques are good in that they can provide a focus to help us reach deep inside and deliver performance beyond the expected. But, visualization is short-term focused with a clear path to the end goal. That is not the **Personal Vision** of this element. To restrict a vision to the steps that can be seen provides a self-limiting element that will hinder breakout performance.

The vision sought in this lesson is seeing a desirable end state so clearly we can communicate it to those who would help us achieve it, even if we don't know how we will do it. I am convinced that the vision of leadership should contain an element of stretch and an element of aspiration that does not allow us to see the steps in between. It must inspire us to attain loftier achievements than we believe are possible in the present. It must leave your area of influence a better place than you found it and a better place for all concerned.

On May 25, 1961, President John F. Kennedy challenged Congress and the nation to land a man on the moon and return him safely to the earth within the decade. This story is legend. Kennedy acknowledged in his speech to Congress that "We have never specified long-range goals on an urgent time schedule, or managed our resources and our time so as to insure their fulfillment."[1] He was stretching his vision and the vision of a nation to achieve what was only a dream by Jules Verne a century before. However, what may not be remembered was that he also asked as a part of this request for the following three additional items:

1) "23 million dollars, together with 7 million dollars already available," to "accelerate development of the Rover nuclear rocket. This gives promise of some day providing a means for even more exciting and ambitious exploration of space, perhaps beyond the moon, perhaps to the very end of the solar system itself."

2) 50 million dollars to accelerate "the use of space satellites for world-wide communications."

3) "75 million dollars, of which 53 million is for the weather bureau," to "give us at the earliest possible time a satellite system for world-wide weather observation."[2]

Jim Collins in his book *Good to Great* calls this a "big hairy audacious goal" or BHAG.[3] In this case, Kennedy had four BHAG's that excited a nation and unified people to a common vision. Whatever you call it, this is stepping out. Three of the four were accomplished; not only revolutionizing space travel, but having far ranging impact on the use of satellites for communication and weather observation in ways which today are taken for granted.

The next obvious question is, "How do I create my own vision?"

The answers are many:

1) It is first important to understand the goals and vision of those who lead you. Even though you may think you know this, I suggest that you take the time for conceptual discussions with them, asking them to articulate their vision and what it means, and to be specific. This is one of the fastest ways to get past the "jargon" and "buzzwords" that cloud communications. It is also one of the fastest ways to see their vision (as well as determining if they have a personal vision) and how you fit into it.

2) Take time for personal reflection. One of the disturbing casualties of our fast-paced life is that we seldom schedule time for personal reflection. There is no immediate benefit, so we put off time for personal reflection and the "important" takes a back seat to the "urgent". But, personal reflection is

imperative in preparation for the next step. Try to think strategically instead of tactically. Think about a desired "end state", instead of concrete goals and the specific steps for achieving them. Dare to think about feelings and soft issues.

3) Discuss what you are trying to accomplish with direct reports and peers to not only bring them on board but also to gain their insight. Hold the same conceptual discussions with them that you may have had with your boss, if you are fortunate enough to have a boss with a **Personal Vision**. In the process, you will be accomplishing for your group what the discussions with your boss did for you. But, remember that your goal is not to let them develop the vision. You are just looking for insight and buy-in to augment your personal reflection. This must be YOUR VISION.

4) Make your vision multi-dimensional. By this, I mean you should not have a narrow focus on something as limited as financial performance. Try to incorporate your personal touch to make a difference. Think past your corporate environment and incorporate what you think will make your group "the best". For example, include elements concerning workplace satisfaction and new technology, while delivering stellar business performance.

5) Look past tomorrow and think 3 to 5 or 10 years into the future. Where do you want to be, and how will you know that you are there?

6) You must believe that this change benefits the common good. One of the first lessons of sales is "you cannot sell it if you don't believe in it". Don't tell your team you are trying to create a new environment if you are only trying to get promoted. They will see through you and nothing will change. As we will discuss in Element 8 (**Take the High Road**), your people look to you to set an example and show them the high moral road. They will help you accomplish your vision much sooner if they believe you are helping them and the team to succeed instead of seeking a personal victory.

7) Keep reinvigorating your vision to keep it fresh. Essentially, you must develop a new vision before you accomplish your old one. This is by far the most difficult part of the process; because, as you progress toward your vision, you need to continually refresh your next 5 to 10 years. It is almost as bad to reach your desired end state and not have something else to lead towards as it is to never have a vision to begin with.

In the end, you will find other aspects that are not covered here. This process is not formulaic. It is more important to start than to wait until you get it right. Your vision will change and improve with time. Reserve the right to get smarter. Just get started.

ELEMENT 2

EFFECTIVE COMMUNICATION

"Even Napoleon had his Watergate."—Yogi Berra

In 1979, as a young engineering supervisor, I met regularly with counterparts managing the operating units to review project backlogs for my engineers. I was only in the job for a couple of months when these peers began to complain regularly about how my engineers were not doing anything. At first, I tried to reason with them by explaining how much the engineers were doing. I became very protective of the members of my team and often vented to my supervisor about how the operations supervisors were being unfair. It took about six months for me to be labeled as "confrontational and defensive". I realized this was not working and could very well limit future opportunities. So, I did some soul searching and had to agree that their assessment was correct. The question, however, remained, "How do I convince the operating supervisors that my engineering team was meeting their needs?" After all, I knew how hard they were working and I knew how much they were accomplishing to meet the supervisors' needs.

Then, one day, I was watching the operating supervisors in their daily rounds. Everyone came to them with information. Everyone, including my engineers, felt that once they told the supervisor verbally what they needed to tell them, their job of communicating was over. The problem was that the supervisors were suffering from overload. So many people informed them verbally of so many things they could not remember it all, and a lot of information was lost.

So, I asked each of the engineers in my group to write a short note at the end of the day and leave it on the supervisor's desk. They were to write down any suggestions they had for improving daily operations, significant progress on a project of interest to the supervisor, answers to questions raised by the supervisor that day, or anything of significance they wanted the supervisor to remember. But, they were to put it on a sheet of paper that the supervisor had to deal with and could not forget.

It took about two weeks for my peers to call me and ask what I had done to get my team motivated. They were excited about the level of support. The engineers were working no harder. They were only putting their thoughts on paper so the supervisor could not forget it. I got lucky. The supervisors responded well to written messages because they were engineers. This may not have worked as well for other audiences. But, in this case it worked because it was a communication style tailored to the recipient.

Lack of good communications is one of the greatest problems facing society as a whole today. It underlies the major difficulties in industry, in marriage relationships, in parent-child relationships, and virtually every place where human interactions take place. At a time when the amount of information we share is increasing at an exponential rate and we have a connectivity that is unparalleled in the history of mankind, we still suffer from poor communication. But, why is that?

Effective communication consists of two elements—(1) understanding the messages sent to you and (2) managing the flow of information to your audience so they get your message.

You first must be willing to listen. Unless people believe you are willing to listen to them, why should they listen to you? Even if you are the boss and have something that you believe your team members need to hear or you have been instructed to deliver, all you will get is benign obedient listening, which will be coupled with personal interpretations at best and lack of retention at worst. Basically, people need to know you care about them and are willing to listen to their concerns, to what is important to them.

But, perceiving their message is much more than just listening. It is also about inquiry and questioning. It is about reading the non-verbal communication to pick up on those clues that help you to understand the spoken word. It is about taking the time to understand all they are trying to tell you. Often the message will be hidden in the words or it may be disguised and diametrically opposed to what you are hearing. Take the time to communicate what you are hearing and ask for clarification to improve your understanding. A good resource to help you hone this skill is to read Habit 5, "Seek First to Understand, Then to be Understood" in Steven Covey's book, *The 7 Habits of Highly Effective People*.[4]

After you have taken the time to listen, you can begin to attempt to communicate your message. To be successful, you must understand that people have a Personal Information Quota, a very deep need for a specific amount of information that they desire from you. This applies to every person with whom you interact—your boss, your peers, your direct reports, your friends, and especially your spouse. We cannot determine what this is for an individual or know in advance what level fulfills their specific need. It will vary by individual. But, it exists and must be fulfilled, so we have a choice to make. We can fill it ourselves and control what fills this quota, or we can leave it up to the individual to fill it. When an individual, any individual, does not have their Personal Information Quota satisfied, they will do one of three things:

1) Add their own interpretation to what they have been told, what they see, and what they hear and make it fit their paradigm.

2) Contact others to obtain information to fill in the blanks. This may be fulfilled by the rumor mill, or it may be another manager sharing more information than you.

3) Assume the information. This is by far the most damaging to your relationship with the listening audience (remember this can be your team, friend, child, or spouse) because the assumptions will seldom be positive. Because they are required to assume the answer, it is normally assumed that the information must be bad or "They would have told us." It will also surprise most managers what people are able to conclude from the few clues that exist in the workplace. We forget that managers do not have the market cornered on intelligence. Most of our workforce is just as capable as we are at deducing logical conclusions from the clues and information readily available. But, this does not mean it will be interpreted in the same light that you interpret it. In the book *Communicating Change*, the authors state, "roughly 40 per cent of employees in the United States, United Kingdom, and Canada report using rumors as a major source of information about the company. You either supply the information the way they want it—face to face—or they go elsewhere for it."[5]

The problem is that most of us do not understand what good communication is. To understand what communication is, it is probably better to look at what it is not:

1) E-Mail—The sheer volume of information passed via e-mail daily is staggering. Most of the time, I feel as though someone is holding a fire hose to my mouth and telling me to swallow. The outcome of the increasing level of correspondence is that I spend more time in my office and less time one-on-one with people in my organization. Unfortunately, these many e-mails often contain large attachments with levels of detail that require considerable effort to digest. This eases the conscience of the sender because he/she "casts their bread upon the waters" and feels they have fulfilled their obligation to "communicate". If I have the time to fully read the notes and attachments, I now must infer their meaning and the consequences to my people.

2) A Lecture—Spending time in the field telling people what they need to hear without listening to their concerns is as fruitless as sending them an e-mail. When you do this, the message is very clear to your team members. You came to deliver your message and they are expected to listen. In the process, not only do you jeopardize the message you intended to deliver, but you alienate your audience and jeopardize any future interaction. Without the ability to participate in a dialogue and test for understanding, it will be difficult to gauge the level of retention or understanding.

3) Telling people only what you have determined that they need to hear—Few things will undermine your

team's trust factor faster than for your team to hear something that impacts them from someone outside your organization. There is a difficult line to manage between guarding confidential information and providing people enough information for them to do their job and to fulfill their Personal Information Quota. This, in itself, impacts their effectiveness on the job. My advice is to err on the side of sharing openly.

I was fortunate to have Major Hal Landrum as an ROTC Instructor at Trinity University. He introduced us to the principle of Napoleon's Corporal. Napoleon kept a corporal at his command station to perform one duty, to read the emperor's battle orders to his generals and to tell Napoleon what the generals were being instructed to do. If the message was clear enough that a front line soldier could understand it, he figured that his generals could not misunderstand it. Napoleon understood that our assumptions, our beliefs, and our subconscious thoughts impact our understanding and we assume our audience has the same perspective. Only by writing his battle orders in a way that they could not be misunderstood could he ensure his commands would be carried out as intended. Today, when we communicate, it is imperative that we test understanding so we don't assume that our audience has all the background we have. Failure to do so leads to ambiguity and interpretation, which causes confusion. A two-way dialogue rich in listening and inquiry is the best way to ensure understanding. Remember, we have only one mouth and two ears. We should talk and listen in that proportion.

But, what should you communicate? The following list is not all inclusive, but it will get your started on your journey.

Communicate Your Vision

First, it is important for your team to understand your **Personal Vision**. You will have to tell them, and tell them, and then tell them again before they begin to believe it and make it a part of their reality. Jack Welch once claimed that 90% of his job was communication. In an article in Business Week in 1998, the author wrote, "In his early years as chief executive, Welch discovered that you can't will things to happen, nor can you simply communicate with a few hundred people at the top and expect change to occur. So he doggedly repeats the key messages over and over again, reinforcing them at every opportunity."[6]

Why is this necessary? For one, people look for consistency. They want to hear your message repeated unchanged so it is not a flavor-of-the-month. They want to see consistency between your words and actions, so they know you believe it and are living it. This is where the greatest challenge to communication arises.

Whenever you make a decision or take action, it is imperative that you communicate openly how this action or decision is consistent with your vision. Your actions or decisions will be judged by your people for consistency with your vision. They are looking for congruency. They want to know if you are "walking the talk?" But, it is a quirk of human nature that any action or decision will be interpreted as violating your vision unless you are in the field actively communicating the link between your actions and your vision to your team. The connection will not always be obvious to them because they don't have your frame of reference and are not privy to all the facts that you had at the time of the action. Failure to do this critical step will undermine the best communication strategy and derail your efforts to get the team behind you. Success at communicating how this link exists will cement your leadership in the minds of your team and make them even more committed to your vision. Repeated follow-up is critical to the success of your communications.

A funny thing happens when you spend the recommended time communicating to your team as I have described. It frees up time that you ordinarily spend handling daily nuisance problems because your team has a better understanding of where you are going and they do not need as much correction or guidance to help you deliver it. It may sound counterintuitive. But, effective, active communication to your team about your vision removes some of the nuisance time from your schedule and allows you to focus on your critical needs.

This is the time for interactive dialogue and listening as you test for understanding. In this way, the interactive dialogue will allow your team to understand and apply the information. We often wonder why another person has trouble understanding our message. After all, it is perfectly clear to me. Why can't they understand? But, we forget that our understanding of a subject is highly influenced by our frame-of-reference and the multitude of subconscious thoughts we harbor related to the matter. It is also highly influenced by our personal filters based on our experiences. It can be interrupted by "hot words" that elicit negative reactions, again based on experiences. The only way you can be sure that communication has occurred is by inquiring and getting your audience to tell you what message they received.

Look for signs that your team is getting the message and acting in support of your vision. Recognize their actions and the word will spread as you build goodwill. In the mid 90's, I was leading an area team on an operating unit and we were trying to implement a participative management work style. We had tried to help our operating personnel understand it was more effective for them to do some minor maintenance than to write a work order for a craftsman to execute. One day while making my morning rounds of the operating area, I observed an operating technician holding and marking the back side of a yellow brush that was used to remove water from the product. He then proceeded to the Maintenance Shop and drilled two holes in the brush. When I approached him and asked what he was doing, he told me that the craftsmen had shown him how to change out the brushes so he would not have to write a work order. He got excited and then commented, "Do you know it costs $ 50 to process a work order?" This was thrilling because it was clear that our message was taking hold. A big smile and a "Thank You" did a lot to recognize him for his work and reinforce the vision.

Communicate Financial Data

A second type of information that is essential to communicate is financial data. This is not an easy task and will take some education of the workforce to be effective. But, the time you spend sharing budget data and financial performance will pay huge dividends to your business performance. Once people understand how they impact the business, they can find ways to help you achieve your vision.

It is important to deliver the information in simple language and avoid the typical corporate buzzwords. It is tempting to use a financial expert to conduct financial training sessions. But, with the first unfamiliar word, the eyes of the trainee will glaze over and you will lose them. Experts in any field will use jargon or terms characteristic of their field and expect everyone to understand them. Worse yet is that the audience will feel stupid for not knowing their meaning. In the mid 90's, I had the good fortune to visit the Training Department of the Caterpillar Assembly Plant in Joliet, Illinois. The two trainers at that site were heritage shop floor personnel (a foreman and a machinist) who had been selected to develop a financial training program in everyday language to share with their peers. Caterpillar consciously avoided degreed financial professionals in favor of putting together a program that people on the shop floor could understand. Six months after completing the training developed from this approach, they were able to document a retention rate for the financial information routinely posted on the shop floor in excess of 90%. Their secret was simple—Make it easy to understand and share openly. The line personnel responded.

There is also a side benefit to sharing financial information openly with your team. It is the first step toward **Personal Empowerment**. And, the trust you build will spill over into other aspects of your work, impacting the three legged stool of Cost Control, Reliability, and HSE (health, safety, and environmental) Performance. It is the first step in building a synergistic approach to performance delivery we will discuss in Element 9, **Think Synergistically**.

Communicating Change

A third type of communication involves anything that impacts people on the shop floor. In their book *Communicating Change* by Larkin and Larkin[7], the authors present an approach to sharing information with the workforce that is counter to the approach normally taken by corporate America. It mainly centers on the effective use of Front Line Supervisors to deliver the information because they know what the people on the front line want to know. The authors build a convincing case that our typical trickle-down approach dooms us from the start because (1) information is power so the middle management filters out some along the way, (2) the majority of the population does not consider nor desire the written word as communication, and (3) we spend time justifying why change is necessary when all they want to hear is how it impacts them. I highly recommend this book to build understanding of the basics of communication to a diverse population and to improve the effectiveness of your communications.

Provide Routine Feedback

As your team finds you approachable, your team members will begin to approach you with questions and make requests. Timely feedback is the fourth type of communication we will cover. Failure to provide timely feedback will undermine your team's belief in you as a caring leader. Remember that in the absence of your information, they will assume answers. You can spend a lot of time trying to answer their questions or meet their needs. But, if you don't provide feedback on what you have been trying to do, they will assume that you have done nothing and don't care about their request. During my last 18 years as a manager, this is the one area that I have been most deficient and the one area on which I would suggest you focus. It has been my experience that you must provide some feedback within 24 hours (preferable the same day if you can) about progress; and then give later feedback to show them that you are pursuing their concern until it is resolved. Give it priority and resolve it quickly. This will keep what is normally considered low priority from cluttering your schedule and build your credibility as a caring leader. This is closely tied to Element 10, **Taking Care of Personnel Matters Expeditiously**.

Failure to provide timely feedback is one of the reasons that entry level professionals, supervisors, and managers alienate their team. If someone on your team comes to you for help on a personal matter, they deserve to know what you are doing about it. Remember that they had to develop enough courage to come to you for help. Telling them you haven't had time to get to it tells them you don't care about them. Telling them you are working on it tells them that you are putting them off. Provide useful, specific feedback that lets them know you either are making progress or provide a reason why you are not pursuing it. And, never tell them you will get them an answer by tomorrow or the next day unless you know you can deliver the feedback. Give yourself ample time to get an answer, but always respond within the window you set.

If someone comes to you about an idea or work request, they deserve to know what you are doing about it. Telling them it is on a project list is like telling them it has been sent to a "No Man's Land". If a front line person cares enough to suggest an idea, they should be kept informed of the progress of their idea or be told that it will not be pursued and the reason it won't be pursued. A major revelation to me was that people will accept a "No" answer almost as quickly as a "Yes" if you show them that you thoughtfully evaluated it and explain your reasons. In most cases, they just want to know that you cared enough to investigate something important to them. My only caution is that a constant diet of "No" will sever any communications. Therefore, be sure to look for the germ of an idea that can be worthwhile.

Provide Performance Feedback

The fifth and final type of communication that is imperative is to provide performance feedback often and specifically. People need frequent feedback, so they know how they are performing and developing and that you value their contributions. We will cover this more fully in Element 3. But, for now, I would like to encourage you to do it often and keep it positive. Tom Kite in his introductory comments to Harvey Pennick's *Little Red Book* said about Harvey that, "Harvey is so careful in choosing what he says that I have often seen him fail to respond to a question until the next day for fear that his answer would be misconstrued. And I can assure you that every answer he finally did come up with was always, always expressed in a positive way. Never would Harvey say, 'Don't do that,' but 'could we try a little of this?'"[8]

Before closing this chapter, it is probably best to review a few common barriers to effective verbal communication:

1) Acronyms—Knowledge is power and understanding what the latest acronym is and what it means is personal power that builds ego. However, this is no different than being the first to have the latest toy, the latest rumor, or the "scoop". Unfortunately, while it may provide the user with a sense of pride or superiority, it sends the message, "I am better or smarter than you." Avoid acronyms. Avoid abbreviations that have become so much a part of our language. Translate them into easy-to-understand terms that cannot be misunderstood. Remember, if your goal is to communicate, you won't do it by using language that your team members don't understand. It is hard work, but your audience will appreciate you for it.

2) Using Technical and Financial Terms—In our quest to educate the workforce, we have shared words or phrases that are commonly understood in technical and financial circles, and we use them as though the audience can understand them because we explained it once six months ago. Engineers and Accountants are the worst. I know because "I are one". Like with acronyms, the goal is to communicate, not turn our audience into technical or financial specialists. Use simple terms, little words, and short sentences that cannot be misunderstood.

3) Failure to test for understanding—No one wants to be labeled as slow or stupid. Some people have even been able to function in business with no reading

literacy by acting like they understand. The same is true if "the Boss" comes to the work place and parrots a new company message but then doesn't test understanding. You may get blank stares or nodding heads, but you will get wasted effort if you don't enter into a dialogue. Ask how this new information applies to their job. Ask what they can do differently. Ask what it means to them. There is no formula to follow or set of standard questions to ask. The point is to begin a dialogue to add substance to the message. Show them you care enough to spend time and help them understand. I once sat in a meeting with two peers I respected. Their boss made a request of them regarding how to improve interactions with support groups in the organization. They came out of the meeting in apparent agreement. But, when I sat with each and we discussed how I could help them to meet their bosses request, I realized their views of what the request meant were 180 degrees out-of-sync. No one took the time to test their understanding and their subsequent actions did little to improve the situation.

4) Not understanding the message yourself and fulfilling an obligation by simply repeating the company line—Sometimes this takes the form of a foreman dropping a letter on a work space and saying, "Read this." Other times, it is a manager reading a presentation and simply parroting the

words on a slide. The message will be clear. You don't understand it. So, how can you expect them to understand it and have meaning?

5) Using charts and graphs to communicate to front line personnel—Most managers in industry are technically trained. They have spent their educational years and most of their career learning and perfecting the art of communicating by charts and graphs. Unfortunately, we assume that everyone learns and communicates as we do. Wrong!!! Nothing will turn off an audience of hourly personnel or front line supervisors promoted from the hourly population faster than relying on charts and graphs to communicate a message. This is unnatural for them. It sends the message that we are smarter or better and you will lose them in the first few minutes.

Communication is not difficult in concept. But, done right, it is the hardest thing you will ever do.

ELEMENT 3

BE A BOUNDARY MANAGER

"Never tell people how to do things. Tell them what to do and they will surprise you with their ingenuity".
—George S. Patton

Most of us were promoted to our first supervisory job due to our Performance Bias (our ability to get things done). From an individual contributor level to a supervisory level, this is more often based on our technical abilities and individual performance than our ability to work with others.

Promotion from a supervisory level to a managerial level is less about the individual technical abilities and more about our ability to work with others. Unfortunately, some people feel the need to get results by micromanaging and telling direct reports how to do their job. After all, we were promoted based on our technical expertise and we need to provide guidance, don't we? This does not always become apparent because at the supervisory level we are still expected (but not required) to have a strong technical background. And, in a performance culture, <u>how</u> results are obtained is often overshadowed by the fact that they <u>are</u> obtained. Micromanaging and telling people how to do their job will only disempower your team members by these actions.

In the early 90's, I had the good fortune to attend a seminar conducted by Johnsonville Sausage Company in Sheboygan, Wisconsin. Ralph Stayer had transformed his company into a model of an empowered organization and the school was offered for others in industry to learn how they had done it. I still remember the revelation from the school that should have been so painfully evident. The instructor told us simply that it is a manager's job to tell people <u>What</u> they want; and, it is the subordinate's job to determine <u>How</u> they do it. So simple! So profound!

Boundary management is the ability to tell people **what** you want (which is a supervisor's real job) and then allowing them the latitude within boundaries that you set to determine **how** they do it (which is their job). The key to effective boundary management is the delicate balance between boundaries so restrictive that they inhibit individualism and boundaries so loose that the results are unacceptable. **In either case, the responsibility for poor results more often lies in a leader's ineffectiveness at establishing clear expectations and good boundaries than in their team's work product**. (Unless you are willing to accept this basic premise, you are wasting your time reading the rest of this lesson.)

The key to providing boundaries that prove effective is in our ability to understand what we want and what we can live with as a final answer. We may not agree with the approach. But, as long as it produces the required results and stays within the boundaries we set, we should be willing to accept the answer and provide appropriate feedback for creative ideas. This is not in the comfort zone for most managers, who tend to micromanage. But the upside is a level of creativity from your people that will surprise you by the results, humble you because you did not think of the answer, and amaze you that it works better than anything you would have done.

If, on the other hand, when we second guess or criticize the approach, we create a culture of people who:

- Leave their brains at the door (60% of the workforce who respond to the environment we create)
- Worse yet, try to figure out how the boss would have done it or wants it done (30% of the workforce who are motivated to do their best to satisfy us).

Lyndon Johnson is often cited for the culture of disempowerment that he created in the Whitehouse. He made all the decision and expected his staff to simply carry out his wishes. During the Vietnam War, he even resorted to personally selecting the bombing targets in North Vietnam.[9] Few people are capable of making all the decisions and always having the right answer. But, what is worse is that this type of disempowering culture will not train your replacement and equip them with the tools necessary to inspire a team to succeed.

Guidelines to Boundary Management:

A. Set clear and specific expectations—Specificity adds clarity—Telling someone to work safely is like telling your child to clean their room. Your definition of clean and theirs will probably be totally different. This sounds so easy and many managers feel that are doing this already. But, it is hard work and it takes time, thought, and effort. The best test of whether you are doing this effectively is to ask your direct reports if they know what you expect of them. It has been my experience in talking with new supervisors and managers that they will candidly say they spent the first six months to a year of their job after being promoted trying to figure out what their boss wants. So ask yourself some simple questions:

1) What specifically do you want?
2) How do you plan to measure compliance with the expectations?
3) How will you know they have reached your expectations? What will it look like?
4) Are the expectations clear in their minds? Can they paraphrase them? (Remember Napoleon's Corporal from Element 2.)

B. Set clear boundaries—

1) What outcome is totally unacceptable to you?
2) Are there budget limits or limits of spending authority?
3) Are there corporate norms or "hot buttons" to avoid?
4) These should be limited to increase space for creativity.

C) Understanding of role (Know your job):

1) Managers determine what they want
2) Subordinates determine how to do it

D) Hold accountable for results

1) Frequent feedback
2) Specific feedback
3) Open-ended questions for understanding, not micromanaging
4) Positive reinforcement for delivering, even if their approach is different than what you expected
5) Celebrate failure as a learning opportunity as long as the failure was the result of well intentioned mistakes and not negligence. Punishing someone for failure instead of celebrating it as a learning opportunity undermines any opportunity for continuous learning. Consider it training cost. An example of this as a benefit will be discussed later in Element 6, **Practice Lifetime Learning**, in discussing Thomas Edison's attitude toward failure.

E) Willingness to accept different approaches—This is the test that will determine if you are serious about creating space for your team. Unless you can accept what was not expected and celebrate the innovation displayed, you will undermine any future opportunity for this to work.

F) Willingness to accept responsibility for results that don't meet your expectations because expectations and boundaries were unclear. After all, you should shoulder the responsibility if the expectations and boundaries were not set properly. You made the mistake, not them.

G) Celebrate Incremental Results—This will require that you stay in touch with the progress of your team members to recognize incremental results. No one ever said you should be hands off. Just remember to stay at the boundaries and let your team tell you how they are making progress. And, then find the opportunity to celebrate progress. It may be a pat on the back, a note to your boss (see Element 7, **Make Heroes of Your People**), or something more significant if the progress is significant. Just find the time to celebrate progress.

If you are unwilling to take the time to identify what specific outcomes you expect and clearly delineate their boundaries, you are comparing and evaluating judgments. Even if you win, you lose.

I will close this chapter with an example from my past where this worked. Our chemical plant had spent an extraordinary effort preparing to transition from a traditional functional organization to a business unit concept where each manufacturing area contained its own operating, maintenance, and technical staff all focused on common goals. I had the good fortune of working with a group that was ready to make the journey; and, within six months of the transition, we had no supervision on shift and the teams were effectively self managing. One day a group of process technicians approached me and asked why we were so restrictive in the number of personnel we allowed to take vacation at the same time.

For a backdrop to this situation, you must understand that our vacation policy was eight pages long and still growing. The reason for the growth was that each year we attempted to close loop holes in the policy to keep people from "taking advantage of the system". In reality, what we were doing was disempowering the workforce by accepting the responsibility to make sure they treated each other fairly. Any absence, whether due to vacation or sickness, caused one of their coworkers to fill their vacancy on overtime. Yet, the current system put supervision in the middle and directed their focus to management and not their responsibility to each other.

After discussing my intention to work with the technicians with the plant leadership team to make sure we were not creating a hardship for another area, I met with the process technicians and offered the following. We would set no restrictions on how many people could take vacation at the same time if they would be willing to meet these boundaries:

1) All shifts would be fully covered.
2) No foreman intervention was allowed.—This put the mutual accountability between coworkers back on them.
3) There would be no increase in cost associated with this.

Within two weeks, they took over their own self management and we never got involved again. And, guess what? We never had an open shift. All we did was treat them as responsible adults and put the accountability where it belonged. We just had to make the boundaries clear.

Supervisors set the boundaries and expectations and coach/mentor people as they work to meet the requirements. This is much harder than it sounds and is a fundamental change from the conventional way of doing business. Understanding your role as a leader will unleash the latent creativity of your people while dramatically enhancing their job satisfaction and self esteem. It will do wonders for employee retention. And, it will make your job a lot more fun when you master your role as a **Boundary Manager**.

CREATE PERSONAL EMPOWERMENT

In 1996, I attended a corporate training program at our central learning campus. During the program, a facilitator led a discussion on the topic of empowerment. We spent two hours allowing middle level management to complain about not being empowered by their supervisor. It was one of the most frustrating meetings of my corporate life. These were potentially some of the most influential managers in our company with the capability to make a huge difference in the performance of the company and they were waiting for someone to tell them to take initiative. I soon realized they were not asking for empowerment. They were asking for delegation. They refused to see that they were guilty of the very shortcoming they were accusing their managers of committing.

If you learn nothing else from this book, this simple personal empowerment process will create space for you to work with reduced oversight and more personal autonomy which should, in turn, make your work more enjoyable and less stressful.

To understand empowerment and accountability, it is important to understand the roles of supervisors and subordinates in an organization. Building an empowered organization starts with the understanding that:

1) A supervisor's job is to determine what needs to be done.
2) A subordinate's job is to determine how they do it.

We covered the role of the leader in Element 3, **Be a Boundary Manager**.

The **Personal Empowerment** side of this equation is that the subordinate's job is to determine how to meet the requirements. It requires a level of personal initiative to take the space created and do something with it. This is where my frustration comes in. You, like me, have no doubt sat in complaint sessions and heard, "My boss will not empower me." It occurs at all levels of any organization. And, it occurs because they misunderstand that we empower ourselves by what we are willing to initiate within our boundaries. **Personal Empowerment** comes from within. Anyone can create **Personal Empowerment** if they follow a simple two-step process:

1) Communicate, communicate, communicate— Open communication fills a void that exists in any relationship (Element 2). In the absence of information, people either create their own information to fill the void, assume the essentials

to fill the void, or seek information. The single greatest favor you can provide for your supervisors is to communicate openly and regularly. This way they know what is happening and how you take care of business. In the process, you create a confidence that you and your team are capable and don't need much supervision. Don't forget to sell the accomplishments of your people to senior levels. It enhances your position as a "bearer of good news" and champion of your people, while you build a positive image of your team and your leadership.

2) Bring solutions, not problems—This is really an extension of the first step. However, in the process of communicating a problem, you want to be known as someone who communicates how they are solving problems, not someone who dumps problems in your supervisor's lap. If you don't want interference, communicate what you are doing. In most cases, your boss will be content to let you proceed while he/she follows up on those who haven't seen the light.

There is not a person in industry today that has not had their area of responsibility expanded to what, at times, seems unmanageable. It makes no difference whether your immediate supervisor is a micromanager or an effective leader. When you follow this process, you free them to focus on their other problem areas. In time, you will find less and less intervention and more opportunity for personal creativity. This works for an individual contributor as well as for team leaders, supervisors, or managers. Stated another way, your boss will stay off your back and provide you a greater range of freedom if he/she has the confidence that your area is being well managed and you have a plan to address problems.

The central issue is one of personal initiative, taking the risk that your solutions are acceptable. We know individuals whose motto is, "It is easier to beg for forgiveness than to ask for permission." They seem to be the ones having all of the fun. An individual who demonstrates the strength of character and initiative to proceed while others are waiting for direction will win and have more fun doing it. The problem is not in our supervisors. The real problem is in us. When we are paralyzed by fear or unwilling to take a risk and expose our judgment to scrutiny by a boss, we lose momentum.

It is also crucial as a leader that you teach and instill this process in your team members. Don't allow them to bring you problems. Discuss these steps and reinforce to them that you will not let them transfer their problems to you. If they try to give you a problem, ask them how they recommend resolving it. Remember that one of your greatest responsibilities is to create leaders for tomorrow. When they leave your tutelage, they carry a subtle message that people from your group are desirable for their self-direction and productivity. You may hesitate to turn over your group too frequently. But, by teaching them and moving them to other areas, you expand your area of influence and create a positive network that is your contribution to benefit your entire organization.

MAKE IT HAPPEN

*"Whether you think that you can,
or that you can't, you are usually right."*
—Henry Ford

At some point in our career, you will be faced with opposition to change. It will come in many forms and from some of your most committed people. They are not bad people; and, in most cases, they are convinced they are helping you by keeping you from making a mistake. These are the times that you have to make things happen. You will hear convincing arguments about why your goals cannot be accomplished. People you respect will advise you to back away. This is a critical turning point. You either make it happen, or nothing will change. This is the mark of true leadership.

The ability to take action is often thwarted by many factors. But, I believe the three most important steps to take to make progress are focus in the face of uncertainty, focus on your real goal, and willingness to take a stand. Each of these will be addressed in the following sections.

"Anxiety is a thin stream of fear trickling through the mind. If encouraged, it cuts a channel into which all other thoughts are drained."—Arthur Somers Roche

Focus in the Face of Uncertainty

Philip Hodgson and Randall White in their book, *Relax, it's only uncertainty,* state "that ambiguity is a place where opportunity exists." They further add that "ambiguity is how it is, and uncertainty is how we feel about it. So, the effective leader is always coping with his or her own feelings of uncertainty in the face of ambiguity."[10] And, they precede this remark with the statement, "the real mark of a leader is confidence with uncertainty—the ability to admit it and deal with it."[11] The book discusses learning how to relax and embrace ambiguity and to lead in the face of our own uncertainty. This book is an excellent resource.

People are hungry for leadership. They are looking for someone who can light the way and lead them through uncertain times. The question is then simple. How can you show confidence and leadership in the face of your own uncertainty?

I believe the key is in recognizing that ambiguity holds both pitfalls and opportunity. And, we can decide on which of these we want to focus. Unfortunately, there is a tendency in industry today to analyze until we can make the pathway clear so we can prevent failure. And, this is fostered by our reluctance to accept well-intentioned mistakes that happen in a learning environment. We lose sight of the fact that it is okay to make mistakes as long we learn from them. Failure to move or make a decision for fear of the pitfalls is a 100% guarantee of failure. The only leaders who win in this race are those that are willing to decide in the face of ambiguity and move forward. Their answers may not be perfect in retrospect. But, like a sailboat tacking into the wind, at least they are directionally correct and moving forward.

So, the only option for a true leader is to embrace our uncertainty and move forward.

The difficult part is to do so with confidence. And, you can do that if you truly believe in the power of your team to help make the way clear. It also helps if you know that your vision is to achieve a higher purpose and is not focused on personal gain. Focus on the pitfalls is paralyzing. Focus on the opportunities is invigorating and leads to breakthroughs.

This is why it is so important to have a clear **Personal Vision** (Element 1). If you know where you want to go and can articulate it to your team, they can help you find the path or a faster way to get to your vision. It just requires focus and commitment on your part. But, it helps you to display confidence, not in having all the answers yourself, but in having faith in your team and their ability to find innovative ways to succeed.

Inspiring leaders often take extraordinary steps to emphasize their commitment to their vision in the face of uncertainty. In

1518, Hernando Cortez was appointed to lead an expedition into Mexico. When he landed on the coast of Mexico with "11 ships, 508 soldiers, 100 sailors, and . . . 16 horses" he founded Veracruz. He then burned his ships to commit his entire force to their goal of conquering Mexico. And, this small band of men conquered a nation of Aztecs numbering over 500,000.[12] He lost only about 200 men in the process.[13]

But, is it necessary for a leader to "burn his ships" in the current political environment of most large companies? I don't believe it is. However, you must have the heart of a barbarian[14] to be a leader. This begins with the simple belief that your quest is imperative and reachable. It begins with you instilling your **Personal Vision** in your team and then taking steps to make it happen. And, you must make it happen. Your team may believe in your vision. They may want to help you. But, if you are not taking steps to break their comfort zone, your vision will be no more attainable than a dream.

I learned a bitter lesson in the early 1990's about making change happen. As I have already mentioned in Element 2, we were attempting to instill a participative management environment in our work place. We were attempting to break the paradigm that required people to leave their brains at the front gate and be told what to do and how to act. We had been organized by business units and given the human resources to make it a reality. We attended seminars and read countless books about the subject and were now trying to bring it to fruition. Unfortunately, at the time, I erroneously believed that the end state was so desirable that if we created the need, created the vision, and offered the opportunity for the end state the team wanted, they would make it happen.

And, was I ever wrong. About four months into the new experiment, nothing was happening. I could not understand why people weren't accepting the challenge and making change. They understood where we wanted to be. They said they wanted to go there. They were excited about the opportunity to use skills that we had denied them in the past. But, nothing was happening. The answer was simpler than the question.

Change is hard. Change will only happen if <u>we</u> make it happen. This was when I learned the hardest lesson of change. Change only happens when it is made imperative. For us, there was a paradox. The change required to adopt a participative management work style would only happen by using some command and control to initiate the change. And, it was really no different than Cortez burning his ships. We worked with our business counterparts and delivered a sobering message to the entire team (operating technicians, craftsmen, loaders, and supervisors) that our current work style was uncompetitive. We could only profitably serve 25% of the marketplace for our products. And, we had a choice to make. We could change our cost structure so we could profitably serve a larger portion of the market or we would be sold. It was a bitter pill to swallow and one not easily accepted. So, we structured meetings with all levels of the team and offered them opportunities to identify changes they could make to improve our cost structure. Real change began to happen. Within two years, we could profitably serve 75% of the marketplace and people were having fun in our new work environment.

About this time, I learned another valuable lesson that helped me focus in the face of my uncertainty. In the spring of 1993, I attended the Industry Week Best Plant Conference in Chicago. During a panel discussion about how the best performing plants achieved their success, I witnessed a revelation from one of the speakers, the plant manager for a Gilbarco plant in the Southeast. He told us that early in their change effort, he invested an inordinate amount of time trying to convince and convert the negative element of his workforce, those who were a negative influence on his change effort. And, then one day, he realized that he never would convert them and that he was wasting his efforts trying to convince them. So, he began to focus all of his efforts acknowledging those who were helping him to make the changes that his business needed. A strange thing happened. The negative element became quiet. They were no more convinced than before. But, the positive feedback to those trying to make a difference was reinforcing the right efforts and bringing in the fringe element that waited to see how things would develop. The lesson was simple. <u>Don't waste time trying to convince the negative element of your workforce</u>. If you can't get rid of them, don't waste time on them. They can only drag you down.

Understand Your True Goal

In order to lead a team effectively, the team members need a clear understanding of the goal of the organization. This occurs at two levels. The first level is discussed in Jim Collin's book *Good to Great* where he described his hedgehog concept.[15] His point is simple that great organizations have a clear understanding of their focus. There must be a clear understanding of what you can (and cannot) be best at and how will you differentiate yourself in a competitive market. And, this is a point that you can make so clear that everyone can rally around it.

But, the second level of this involves how you set goals and performance metrics within the departments and groups of an organization. In his book, *The Goal*, Eliyahu Goldratt does a masterful job of explaining that we can become so engrossed in the job of doing our job that we lose sight of our true goal.[16] At first blush it seems simple. Our goal is to make money. But, as we begin the process of setting goals below a corporate level, we begin to see the emergence of conflicting goals that set department against department, plant against plant undermining the opportunity for true collaboration and decreasing our productivity. For example, it is not uncommon for a Maintenance organization in support of Operating units to have goals that are well-intentioned around the productivity of individual craftsmen and the department as a whole, assuming they can contribute to the success of the company and their plant by improving their productivity. But, if that productivity causes inefficiencies in the Operating areas through reduced unit availability or ineffective use of raw materials, the gains in Maintenance productivity create huge deficits in Operations' productivity and the net result is a loss for the company as a whole.

Now please don't understand this example to mean that Maintenance or other support organizations are the reasons for losses in complex organizations. Their goal to achieve productivity improvements is well intentioned and I have yet to meet a Maintenance Manager whose heart is not in the right place. What I am saying is that no individual portion of an organization can claim to contribute to the efficiency of an organization by optimizing their area in a vacuum, or without understanding the impact of their productivity program on the rest of the organization. Most complex petrochemical manufacturing sites plan their unit operations through the use of a Linear Programming model. The answers are never obvious and one quickly learns that the obvious optimization of a portion of the plant does not lead to the optimum answer for the whole plant. The same is true with individual optimization of a department within a plant, or a team within a department. There are no easy answers to this, but resist the urge to establish goals or measures that prevent other portions of the organization from doing their job. Focus objectives and metrics around your true goal. And, to do that you have to understand what it is.

Take a Stand

With the first two elements above in place (Focus in the Face of Uncertainty and Understanding Your True Goal), you are ready to take a stand. This will be much harder by far, and you will most likely feel very alone, isolated from your team in a suspicious way. But, unless you are willing to take a stand when it is necessary, nothing will change. Worse, yet, if you are unwilling to take a stand, your people will lose respect for your leadership.

When I say, "Take a stand," I mean that at some point in your career, you will be faced with a change that needs to happen. Those around you will, in good conscience, tell you it cannot be done or it takes more time. They will formulate convincing arguments about how this is too much too soon. One leader in our company referred to this as making a "seemingly unreasonable demand". This comes when you know that change must happen. You know in your heart that it is the right thing to do. And, those around you are finding every way possible to keep it from happening. That is the time that you have to drive a stake in the ground and make both your demand and the timing clear. Cortez did this when he burned his ships.

It is difficult to go against the advice of those you have respected and trusted. You have to keep in mind that they are often influenced by being too close to the action. They hear the concerns of those who don't understand what is happening and they know them to be good people. They see their teams being pushed to the limits and are concerned for them. However, they may also become so myopic in their view of what is happening that they lose sight of alternatives that can make it happen. Taking a stand and making it happen is like breaking a logjam and forcing your team members to look at the problems in different ways. It is forcing them to realize that we cannot solve the old problems by trying the same things that did not work in the past.

When you do take a stand, expect a certain initial level of bewilderment. Your team members will not believe you are serious. This is the time to make it clear that you mean business and will not accept any other outcome. It is a time to provide encouragement and support, to let your team know that you believe they can make this happen. The result will often be an innovation that will amaze you. Great things happen when people are tested and given an opportunity to elevate themselves and their team with their accomplishment. The end result is not only accomplishment of your goal; it is the sense of pride and accomplishment felt in your people as they do what they did not think could be done, in less time than they thought. You allow them to be better than they thought they could be.

To conclude this chapter, we are asking you to do three things:

1) Recognize ambiguity and your uncertainty for its opportunities
2) Understand your goal and how you impact the rest of your organization
3) When you know what must be done, **Make It Happen**.

PART II

HOW TO DO IT

ELEMENT 6

PRACTICE LIFETIME LEARNING

"The man who does not read good books has no advantage over the man who cannot read them."
—Mark Twain

Life is simple. You are either growing or you are dying. You are either challenging your mind and body and soul to become smarter or stronger or you are becoming diminished. As we said in Element 5, change is hard. But, to misquote Tom Hanks who played Jimmie Dugan in *A League of Their Own*, "It's supposed to be hard. The hard is what makes it great." And, I can add that it is the change that keeps us growing. To make that change happen requires an attitude of continuous learning; the ability to seek knowledge, the will to continually test our paradigms, the desire to learn from others, and the belief that our current knowledge is just that—the current knowledge.

I was fortunate to be raised in a family that valued a sharp mind. We were always working puzzles, or testing each other with a new mind game. And, to this day I value a good puzzle, quiz or game to keep my mind sharp. A sharp mind is a critical element of the pursuit of knowledge. For that, I will always be thankful to my father, who valued a sharp mind and kept his that way until he died just short of his 82nd birthday.

This book is peppered with references to books by authors whose concepts have made an indelible impact on me. And, I can scarcely remember a single book, seminar, or training course that has not left me with new ideas. I guess I have been fortunate that my life has been a series of revelations, as new concepts have been presented and have helped me to understand the shortcomings of my previous knowledge. This book is my attempt to pull all of these revelations together into a tapestry or model that makes sense to me; one that I can share with others so they don't have to repeat any of my mistakes.

All I can say is never stop learning. You don't have to believe all you read. You may get only one idea or revelation from any book you read or seminar you attend. But, if you can get just one germ of an idea from each source you tap, the journey is worth it. The key is to incorporate each learning into your own personal patchwork and identify how the new insights support or modify your previous understanding. The beauty of knowledge is that if we reserve the right to get smarter, we can maintain an open mind and continue to learn.

One sad bit of learning came from the book *Communicating Change*. In the process of explaining why written communication is ineffective in reaching front line personnel in companies, the authors state, "Only 35 percent of Americans have read a book since graduating from high school, and only 20 percent say they have ever been in a bookstore."[17] If that assertion is true, the need for continuous learning is even more imperative. We can ill afford wasting the opportunity to learn from others and stretching our minds.

Now, do not misunderstand this admonition for continuous learning. That does not mean that we cannot read for pleasure. In fact for each business related book I have read in the last ten years, I have probably read ten fictional novels. The key is to not compartmentalize our reading, but to look for opportunity to learn even from your pleasure, or light reading.

Our company used to hold annual Management Learning Center gatherings for all middle and senior level leaders. A prerequisite for these courses was to read selected books and articles so we came with a common background. One of the books selected was *Managing on the Edge* by Richard Tanner Pascale.[18] It focused on the need to use conflict to stay ahead by bringing people into our team who did not think like you. The idea was to force conflict to broaden the information available and encourage better decision making.

This concept was not new to me because I am a fan of Steven Coontz, who authored the Jake Grafton series. In the book

Under Siege, Jake Grafton held a key leadership position in the CIA and needed broader thinking to thwart a potential nuclear attack on Washington. He brought in a team member whose political and social views were diametrically opposed to his for the sole purpose of broadening the information available to his team. The book addresses the conflict and tensions that ensued. But, it showed the genius of this type of diverse and inclusive thinking. Yet, it was all a backdrop to the story line and played out against the bigger international tensions.[19] It was a revelation for me, and it came from my pleasure reading.

So, keep an open mind. You never know from what direction your next revelation will find you. Read. Discuss. Be Open to learn. So, I offer the following opportunities to learn:

1) Celebrate well intentioned failure and learn from your mistakes.

The following story is told about Thomas Edison:

"On the night of December 9, 1914, Edison Industries was destroyed by fire. The loss exceeded $2 million, along with the vast majority of Thomas Alva Edison's work. Edison was insured for only $238 because the buildings were constructed of concrete, which at that time, was thought to make a building fireproof. At sixty-seven years of age, Edison watched his life's work go up in flames.

"The next morning, after firefighters had finally brought the inferno under control, Edison surveyed his charred dreams and crushed hopes. As he surveyed the scene, he said, 'There is great value in disaster. All our mistakes are burned up. Thank God we can start anew.'

"Three weeks after the fire, Edison Industries produced the first phonograph.

"In every setback one can find the seeds of a future success. Such a success, however, will not be automatic. One must plant those seeds with vision, fertilize them with hope and hard work, and continue to water them with enthusiasm."[20]

Oh, that we could all have the positive attitude of Edison. He did not consider it recovering from a major setback. He saw it as wiping the slate clean of his old mistakes, learning from them and using them as a springboard for new opportunity.

Unfortunately, it is easier to view our failures in a negative light and view mistakes of those who report to us as failures. We must also treat the well intentioned mistakes of our team as an opportunity to learn. We must remember that no one will make all the right decisions every time. Progress is made by moving forward and learning from the mistakes of the past, and being right at least 51% of the time. Instead of berating yourself and your team for the mistakes of the past, celebrate them as learning experiences and your team will respond. This is an investment in the future of your team.

2) Learn by sharing with others.

One major reason we read is to learn from others. Most authors who write books on management philosophy or leadership were not born with the answer. Most of them conducted extensive research to learn from experts in the field about their mistakes and successes. I suspect that like me they had a revelation or series of revelations that they felt compelled to share with others. Learning is about talking with others about what worked and did not work for you and listening to their stories. Experiences are often situation related. And, by discussing with others who have traveled a similar journey, you can help to see if things did not work because your thinking was flawed or if it was because some unforeseen influence kept it from working.

Sharing with others also helps you to better understand what is happening with your team. There is something about verbalizing your thoughts that helps you to make sense of them. The very process of sharing with another not only gives you another perspective, it also helps you crystallize your path forward. Learn to share openly.

One way to share with others is to have conceptual discussions about leadership with your peers about your supervisor's vision and their **Personal Vision**. Spend time talking about what terms like empowerment mean to them. In the process of these discussions, you gain a better and more common understanding of terms that are often ambiguous. The time will be well spent.

3) Seek a mentor.

This is not mandatory and you can succeed without one. But, if you have the good fortune to find someone who will take you under their wing and guide you, the help is invaluable. Leadership can be lonely. It is hard to discuss our uncertainties or things that confuse us with our teams without undermining their faith. Every leader could benefit from a mentor to help them see their own shortcomings and opportunities for improvement.

But, there is one word of caution. A mentor is not all knowing. Find someone you trust and respect. Find someone with whom you can be open and honest. Just don't follow them blindly. Use them to guide you. Evaluate their counsel. But, in the end, be true to your heart. It is easier to be an advisor than someone with a stake in the game. The decisions and actions are yours, not your mentors. Make the hard decisions. Take the necessary action. Believe in yourself.

4) Don't carry the baggage of past mistakes.

As a veteran of 34 years in the petrochemical industry, I have had the chance to look back on my life, often with regret for past mistakes. I cannot go back and change them, as much as I would like. I can only learn from them and accept them for what they are—a part of what made me who I am today. The brashness of youth leads to the daring leadership of tomorrow. The passion of yesterday helps mold the colorful character of today. Accept the past and look to the future.

MAKE HEROES OF YOUR PEOPLE

As much as people desire a leader they admire and respect to follow, they also want to be appreciated for their efforts. A leader who makes heroes of his people taps a need in the soul of his followers that cultivates devotion and loyalty. By foregoing your ego and recognizing the contributions and sacrifices of those responsible for making your vision a reality, you win their hearts and forge a team that will accomplish extraordinary things.

The journey to making heroes of your people begins with the understanding that it is not about you, it is all about them. If you are leading a team because you want to look good, they will see through your veneer and become disenfranchised. If you are leading a team because you are trying to fulfill a personal agenda, your team will soon realize that there is nothing in it for them. But, if you believe that what you are doing fits a higher purpose and that you are only providing direction for a great group of people, they will sense it and make the effort (often a quantum leap) to great performance.

To make heroes of your people, you have to communicate up and down the organization, as well as with your peers. People who enjoy their work are anxious to tell you what excites them about their job. Quite often, they are looking for the chance to tell you what they have done that gives them pride and distinguishes them in the job. But, first they have to know that you genuinely care about them and want to hear about what they are doing that excites them. This is where effective dialogue from Element 2 comes into play. By interacting, asking what is going on in their lives, and by providing positive reinforcement for their achievements, they will share the good things that are happening.

And, when they do, you have a choice to make. You can acknowledge their work and provide positive reinforcement and stop there. Or, you can send the message of their accomplishments to your boss and to their peers. You can make heroes of your people. It won't take long for them to know that you are "bragging" about them, that you are proud of them. They may even want to downplay their accomplishments. But, deep inside, they will truly appreciate your recognizing them in this way and strive harder to find ways to make you proud. By doing this, you tap into fundamental human emotions and satisfy the need to be appreciated. By doing so, you build a loyalty base that is powerful.

But, you also do something else. By telling good news stories about your people, you become known in your organization as a bearer of good news. You increase the positive perception of your team. In short, you become known as someone who cares about your people.

All this begins by being in their space. You have to be approachable. You have to be seen as caring. You have to be seen as someone who feels they are worth spending time with. When you do, they will open up, first about inconsequential daily work matters. Maybe they will test you with a request to investigate something for them or explain something to them. But, soon they will talk about more personal things. They will talk about family. They will ask about your family. They will begin to share their concerns, and may even talk about their secret passions and hobbies. As long as you show genuine concern and interest, the trust level builds and they will continue to be more open. Cherish this and build on it.

ELEMENT 8

TAKE THE
HIGH ROAD

*"Nearly all men can stand adversity, but if you want
to test a man's character, give him power."*
—Abraham Lincoln

I once attended a training seminar titled Effective Process Supervision. The seminar leader, Bill Tillman, made the statement that if a group does not like the leader appointed to them, they will elect a natural leader from the group. He further commented that they will select someone who is aloof. I recorded that in my notes and have pondered for years to understand it more fully. At first, I interpreted this as meaning that people instinctively want a leader who does not form relationships that would compromise their objectivity as a leader. They want someone who will be fair to all parties involved. And, I still believe this logic is valid.

But, after years of observing people and working with teams, I am convinced that this is just the tip of the iceberg. People want more. They want a leader with a strong moral character, someone they can count on to take care of them and represent their interests. They want someone who will **Take the High Road**.

Now you are probably asking, "What does this mean?" What is taking the High Road? And, before you can answer this question, you have to ask yourself, "What are my moral convictions? What is it that I would be willing to take a stand on as a leader?" And, as you answer these two questions, you will need to understand that this is about more than your religious affiliation or religious beliefs. It is about how you conduct business and treat people. It is about your core values.

The simplest test is the proverbial red face test—Do you get up in the morning and feel good about the person you see in the mirror? After making a business decision that forces you to choose between employee concerns and bottom line profit, can you look at yourself in the mirror and feel good about the person you see?

But, the true test is in how you respond to the challenges that you will experience. The people on your team will test your commitment to **Take the High Road**. It is not because they are immoral. It is not because they really want or expect you to compromise your principles. They are just looking for positive reinforcement that you will maintain your high moral standards. It is reassuring when you demonstrate that you are not willing to compromise your standards. They need the reassurance.

But, first you must establish an environment that values high moral standards. To do this, you can follow these guidelines:

1) Set expectations

   When you set expectations for your team (Element 3), voice your values and expectations on moral issues. This may sound archaic. But, people need to know up front what you will and will not tolerate. They need to know that you are unwilling to compromise your principles.

2) Discuss moral issues when discussing business direction.

   As part of any discussion concerning business direction, openly share your views on the moral issues as part of the discussion. If you have an open meeting and encourage brainstorming, there will probably be suggestions that are counter to your values, if not borderline illegal. Try to encourage all the open ideas that can be generated. Wait until after the brainstorming session, then be open to your team about why these ideas concern you and are not acceptable. Be sure to only do this during the evaluation phase to keep the atmosphere open. The trick is to do so with respect, as a father guiding a child and helping them to learn. Remember that this is a necessary part of the challenge phase. This will help to reinforce your commitment to your values.

3. Counsel your team members when their actions or comments are inappropriate.

   In most cases, this will come in the form of an errant comment in a meeting. It may be in jest. Or, it may be sincere. What is important is that you make your concerns clear. Do so with respect. Do so with diplomacy. But, do so sincerely, so there is no question of where you stand.

   If the actions of a member of your team are inappropriate, counsel them privately about your concerns and explain why they are not consistent with the culture you are building. People need to know where you stand.

Taking the high road cannot be faked. Insincerity will be exposed. It must be a part of your life, not just your work life.

People want and need to see us **Take the High Road**.

THINK SYNERGISTICALLY

"Choose always the way that seems the best, however rough it may be. Custom will soon render it easy and agreeable."
—Pythagoras

Industry today suffers from Initiative Overload. We are asked (1) to achieve better safety performance, (2) to achieve ISO 14011 certification, (3) to achieve ISO 9000-2000 certification, (4) to improve our reliability, (5) to achieve cost leadership in a competitive market, and all the other initiatives that seem to come our way (you fill in the blanks). Some are industry driven. Many are corporate driven by some well meaning Senior Leader who thinks his new idea will assure compliance and achieve greatness. At least it sounded good when he presented it to the Company leadership. For whatever reason, the brunt is felt by the local leader asked to implement this spaghetti bowl of requests.

The problem with this divided approach is that we tend to think of initiatives such as these as individual efforts that must be handled separately. And, this approach leads to conflicting priorities and confusion. Today, we talk about safety and tomorrow we talk about productivity or cost. The message is that each is a flavor-of-the-day (or moment) and we are confused and overworked, our people are confused and overworked, few things get completed as designed, and we all feel anxious at our mediocre achievements.

But, there is a better way. It is about thinking synergistically. Imagine, if you will, that each problem you encountered was evaluated in the context of meeting multiple needs before agreeing to a plan going forward. Imagine, if you will, that instead of developing your site safety plan, or reliability plan, or environmental compliance plan, ad nauseum, that your needs for compliance in each area were seen as values to be satisfied in each stage of your work. At this point, you no longer have competing priorities that make you argue about cost versus production. Instead, you have a plan that satisfies all your needs while providing the safest, lowest cost, more environmentally friendly, most reliable solution.

This is the role of the synergistic leader. Instead of wasting time addressing all the myriad of demands separately, he or she shields their team from this quagmire and guides them to synergistic solutions. In the process, not only is the leader creating world class performance, but they are also developing leaders for the future, which is one of the most overlooked roles of a leader.

The question is how to break the cycle of separate priorities and begin to think and act synergistically. To make this happen requires conscious thought and the recognition that the old paradigm will not get you where you want to be. So as a starting point, I suggest the following actions:

1) Take time for quiet reflection to identify all the demands on your time. You can begin by listing all the initiatives that mire you down. The list will be daunting.

2) Identify the commonalities of these demands. I suspect you will find that there is a high level of redundancy and you are doing the same thing several times to satisfy different initiatives.

3) Create the values that will drive your decision-making and capture them in a list. The list does not have to be all inclusive, as long as you consider the list dynamic and you are willing to modify it as you get smarter.

4) Communicate your intentions to your direct reports. They will be confused if they see you doing something different and won't understand why.

5) Stop compartmentalizing your decision making and integrate your list of requirements in each decision so your list of values has been satisfied before you proceed.

6) Guide your team to think about an integrated decision-making model as a method to teach them to be better leaders.

TAKE CARE OF PERSONNEL MATTERS EXPEDITIOUSLY

"Be quick, but don't hurry."
—John Wooden

If you want your team to know that you care about them, handle personnel matters expeditiously. We tend to think of personnel matters as a nuisance job of management and put them off until we have to take care of them. Delays handling personnel matters send a clear message that we don't believe the people involved are worthy of our time and efforts.

Personnel matters take many forms. They can be assisting an individual to solve a problem, staffing issues, addressing interpersonal conflicts on your team, disciplinary matters, etc.

Staffing Issues

In his book, *Good to Great*, Jim Collins presents a convincing argument about making sure you have the right team in the Chapter "First Who . . . Then What".[21] His point is that you need to make sure you have the right people in the right role before trying to decide what you are going to do. Make the tough decisions to have the right people in the right roles and get rid of the wrong people. Most of the examples in his books describe efforts of successful CEO's to get their team right. But, this concept applies to all levels of an organization, from the CEO to the front line.

Ineffective people disrupt the productivity of everyone around them. In the example on disciplinary matters that follows this section, an hourly employee created disruption for his shift crew, his supervisor, his supervisor's supervisor, and this supervisor's supervisor's supervisor. All the way up the line, this occurred because someone was unwilling to get the wrong person out of a role. Failure to address the wrong person simply created a hardship for coworkers that they didn't deserve. As a result of failing to take care of a problem early, the problem festered, morale suffered and employees were led to believe that management did not care. Make the tough call and your remaining team (the survivors) will thank you and respect you for caring about them.

Handling Disciplinary Matters

At a manufacturing location that I came to manage, a problem was identified with an hourly employee. His actions had almost created an environmental incident and had cost us loss of raw materials. On further investigation, it was clear that the employee in question had a history of documented performance problems.

We initiated disciplinary action commensurate with the infraction and eventually had to escalate the disciplinary action later, which led to the employee's termination. The day after his termination, one of the other plant operating technicians (who I respected for his attitude and work ethic) approached the site supervisor and told him, "It took you guys long enough." His team had felt like they were carrying him for years and had been waiting for "supervision" to do something about it. We thought we acted prudently and consistent with the requirements of the disciplinary policy. But, the plant personnel were frustrated it took so long for us to address his deficiencies.

During the preparation for termination, we reviewed his personnel history and found his probationary evaluation from his first six months in the plant. He had been rated below average and the foreman who completed the evaluation had recommended termination during the probationary period. His site supervisor at the time overruled his recommendation because it would take too much time to hire a replacement. This problem could have been handled quickly and prevented a lot of grief for other site personnel if it had been handled when his performance issues were first recognized. Instead, due to a decision to live with a problem and not address a personnel matter expeditiously, the previous supervisor created a hardship for everyone who worked with the employee for several years. In the process, he created an impression that we did not care and would tolerate poor work performance.

I have had to fire many people in my career, unfortunately. It is never an easy task and it is one that I do not approach lightly. However, one revelation that has come to me is that failure to handle a situation quickly creates a hardship for coworkers, which is not fair to them. So you have to make a choice. You either tolerate poor work performance and create a problem for the rest of the offender's team, or deal with the problem. I can safely say that in all cases that eventually led to someone's termination, a problem had been identified and recorded during their probationary period. A prompt decision could have saved me and the company a lot of grief.

Failure to address personnel matters expediently will quickly undermine your credibility as a leader.

Addressing Interpersonal Conflicts on Your Team

One of the greatest mistakes that I have made as a leader was failure to address interpersonal conflict among members of my immediate staff. This is often the most frustrating of all personnel matters because it will normally involve good people, who simply don't work well together. They may be highly rated individually. But, if they cannot work effectively as a team, their actions will clearly be understood by your whole organization as fighting factions instead of team members working together. And, worse, you will be clearly to blame. The impact on your entire team will be unrest, low productivity, fighting and dissention, confusion and anxiety, and eroding employee morale across the entire organization.

This is not an easy one to solve. You need to make your expectations clear and hold a tough love intervention meeting with fighting members. You will also have to send a very strong message that failure to resolve the conflict will force you to make changes. Team building efforts seldom address this level of conflict. Whatever you do, you must make it clear that they are seen as a cohesive team or you will bring someone else in to do it. This is not a time to let individual performance cloud your thinking. For as your team progresses up the managerial chain, they must learn to work with others to achieve success.

Assisting An Individual to Solve a Problem

It takes a lot of contemplation for most people to approach a supervisor to help them solve a problem. In most cases, they have attempted to get it resolved with increasing frustration. Coming to a supervisor is often seen as a last ditch effort and an admission of failure on their part. The last thing they need is for you to give their needs a low priority. This only confirms their low opinion of themselves (after all they failed to handle the situation before coming to you and had to humble themselves to seek your help). However, it also sends a clear message of their worth to you and to the company if you respond quickly and decisively.

In most cases, they will be looking for help to navigate ambiguous policies and procedures; some that may even frustrate you. What they deserve is a quick response to indicate that you have begun investigating their concern. The same day is preferable, but within 24 hours is acceptable. And, if your initial investigation cannot resolve their concerns, give them an estimated date to finish handling their concern. Then, make sure that you address it. And, if the future date is too far out (a month or two); provide them interim feedback so they know that you are working on it. This goes back to the initial rule of communication. If you don't let them know what you are doing, they will assume that you are either doing nothing or whatever you are doing is not effective.

Also, do not hesitate if the answer is, "No." People first want an answer and will accept a well researched and carefully considered negative answer, as long as you believe this is the right answer and explain your rationale sincerely. Delaying your response because it is unpleasant to say "No" is far worse because you will be seen as uncaring and ineffective. People will accept any response as long as they know why.

One of the best leaders that I experienced was very effective at addressing employee concerns expediently. He was not highly respected for his technical knowledge. But, his team loved to work for him because he took care of their concerns quickly and showed them he cared. This was a lesson learned early that paid big dividends.

ＥＬＥＭＥＮＴ 11

SHARE YOUR PASSION

"It's kind of fun to do the impossible."
—*Walt Disney*

People trained for technical and financial disciplines are notorious for being so focused on their work that they can appear almost mechanical and inhuman. These disciplines tend to attract people who are more introverted, who tend not to show their emotions easily and therefore appear dispassionate. Dispassionate behavior inhibits effective leadership.

Don't misunderstand what I am saying. This is not an argument that leaders must be extroverts. All I am saying is that it is okay, even desirable, to let your team see you displaying passion and eagerness about your work. The trick is to do it in a positive way that helps them to become and stay invigorated. Let them know that it is okay, even desirable, to get excited and enthusiastic about their work.

The first step to sharing your passion is to know what your passion is. You may know already or you may have to contemplate what excites you. Just knowing that you enjoy what you do is not enough. Take the time in quiet reflection to analyze what it is that drew you to your vocation/job/company. Note when you were the happiest and most productive in your work. What got you excited? But, it is not enough to know what excites you. It is also necessary to understand why you have this passion. Again, take time in quiet reflection to gain this understanding. This is necessary for two reasons. First, you cannot share your passion until you know what it is. And, second, you cannot communicate your passion effectively until you know why it excites you. People will ask and you need to be ready to communicate effectively.

Now, you are ready to let your passion shine forth. It cannot be forced or it will appear insincere. All you are really doing is let your excitement show without hiding your feelings. If your team is confused by this sudden change in your demeanor, now is the time to explain to them why you love your job and what it is about it that excites you.

Then, take the opportunity to ask your team members what it is about their job that arouses their passion. Sit and listen. Ask questions for clarification so you not only understand, but also show them that you care and want to know more about them.

Above all, let your passion shine and you will be surprised how much better you feel about your day.

ELEMENT 12

HAVE FUN

Several years ago, after a young supervisor moved from our facility to another location, she and I happened to attend a management training session for a week. We spent each day discussing concepts, engrossed in continuous learning with an extended team of managers from across our business sector. The mood was much lighter than at work and there was a lot of joking and teasing between areas of the company. I did what I normally do in that environment and joined in with frequent jokes and humorous comments. After about four days of the training course, the supervisor approached me and told me that she never knew I could be so much fun to be around. That comment came like a kick in my stomach because she was really telling me that I was stodgy and rigid at work and needed to lighten up. And, she was right.

One of the common misconceptions held by many leaders is that they have to maintain an authoritative presence; that they have to maintain a dignified and wooden appearance. In the process, they appear very intense and focused but not having much fun. And, that is sad. What is even sadder is that this is done to maintain control. Herb Kelleher was once asked by a financial analyst if he was afraid of losing control of his organization. He responded that he never had control and never wanted it. "If you create an environment where the people truly participate, you don't need control. They know what needs to be done, and they do it."[22] I believe this is why Herb is able to let go and have fun. Hire the right people and you don't have to be in control.

We need to let people know that it is okay to **Have Fun**, that it is okay to joke at work, and that work can be fun. The brief interruptions may seem counter to your perception of productivity. But, you soon realize that breaking the monotony and allowing people time to unwind improves overall productivity because they feel better about what they are doing, about themselves, and about you. And, the emotional release of an occasional laugh reduces the tension that limits our overall productivity. When Colleen Barrett was an EVP at Southwest Airlines before succeeding Herb as President, she was quoted as saying they are looking "for a sense of humor, a sense or service, and we screen out bad attitude."[23] The leadership of SWA obviously realizes that humor in the workplace is an advantage not to be avoided.

But, the next question you will probably ask is how can I lighten up and be taken seriously? How can I joke at work and be respected? I think the key to understanding is in realizing that as a leader you set the tone for your group. Herb Kelleher was a noted jokester. He set a humorous, light-hearted tone in

Southwest Airlines and demonstrated that it is okay to have fun. He knew that instead of undermining productivity, a happy environment energizes people and encourages them to treat each other and customers with greater dignity.

But, there is another aspect of humor in the workplace that needs description. I learned long ago that by teasing my team members with gentle gibes and encouraging them to tease me, "the boss", we created a more open environment. This led to more open discussions and less resistance to discuss concerns, bear bad news, and the like. It also helps to find humor in tense situations in order to break the tension and set your team at ease to deal with problems. Humor is good, and used judiciously, it improves the work environment and builds morale.

The real key to effective humor in the workplace is to avoid malicious humor. Your goal is not to have fun at the expense of one of your team members. So, there are a few simple rules:

1) Don't be afraid to be the butt of the jokes. It is okay for others to laugh at you. In fact, you can initiate this behavior by telling your team about your humorous mistakes and failures. It makes you more human. It makes you more approachable. It makes you someone they want to be open with. And, it does not undermine your authority. That is why Herb Kelleher makes himself the butt of the joke in front of countless employees of Southwest

Airlines. He realizes that a happy workplace is more productive. And, it is more important for people to enjoy their work, than for a leader to maintain a facade of control.

2) Laugh! Laugh when others tease you in a good natured way. Laugh when you tell a funny story about yourself. Laugh when someone tells an appropriate joke. It is important for your team to see you having fun at work. It is important for them to see you enjoying yourself and what you do. It helps people feel appreciated.

3) Never, never, never, never tell a story that makes a counterpart in another portion of your company the butt of your joke in an attempt to bring humor to the situation. This will only encourage your team to make others the butt of inappropriate jokes. But, even more importantly, it will make you appear as less of a team player in their eyes. If you insult one co-worker, you insult them all.

4) Give positive feedback when someone uses humor appropriately, whether they are teasing you and got the better of you or they tell a funny story on themselves. You need to make it clear that you appreciate and encourage appropriate humor.

After that, just **Have Fun**.

REMAIN CALM
IN CRISIS

"If you can keep your head when all about you are losing theirs
and blaming it on you, . . . you'll be a Man my son."
—*Rudyard Kipling*

The ability to remain calm in a crisis allows you to be objective, to assess the situation accurately, to seek necessary input from those more knowledgeable, and proceed with an action plan that has the greatest opportunity for success.

As a young manager in my first leadership position, I violated this principle repeatedly. At the time, I mistakenly thought that action was necessary as a sign of leadership. At the first sign of crisis, I would assemble all my direct reports and begin to take action without benefit of proper evaluation, reacting only on gut feelings. My family worried about me and begged me to calm down for fear that I would have a heart attack. My team looked at me in confusion because I was reacting and not leading and this instilled little confidence. As a consequence, our response was slower and less effective than if I had taken to time to step back calmly and assess the situation before beginning action.

I don't know when the transformation occurred. But, in later years just before retiring, one of my direct reports told me that he had always admired the way I remained calm in a crisis because it helped the whole team slow down and act responsibly. At the same time, I realized that I was having a whole lot more fun at my job.

But, this begs the question, "How do you develop the ability to **Remain Calm in a Crisis**?" For me, the following is necessary to develop this ability and to maintain it for future use:

1) Resist the urge to react—This is not a hockey game or fire fight in a battle in which you have trained to act on instinct. You may eventually find that your initial thoughts are correct. But, hold back and let a cooler head prevail. You set the tone for your team and if you want them to act rationally, you must set the example.

2) Resist an emotional response—Excitement or anger will trigger a similar response in those around you and prevent you from maintaining objectivity. You must be the source of reason and calm. Take a moment to realize these feelings if they occur and recognize them for what they are—feelings that are neither good nor bad. They are just feelings,

not an excuse to succumb to them. *"A gentle answer turns away wrath, but a harsh word stirs up anger."*— *Proverbs 15:1*

3) Speak slowly—There is a natural tendency in a crisis situation to speed up your speech in reaction to the adrenaline rush you may no doubt experience. Speaking quickly makes it harder for others to understand you and to comprehend your meaning. Even though it is true that people can hear at a rate that is 5 to 6 times faster than you can talk, there is an emotional element in talking too quickly that is communicated as well. Remember that 90% of communication is non-verbal. Learn to speak slowly to calm yourself and your team, especially in the face of crisis.

4) Determine the safety of the people and surrounding impacted area as a first priority—This must be genuine, for the team will know if it is not. It helps immensely if your team is accustomed to this being your first priority. Once your team knows that your heart is in the right place, they will move heaven and earth to help you resolve the crisis.

5) Determine the source of the crisis—Ask probing questions of those around you who probably have more information on the subject than you. Resist the urge to place blame. Create an environment that encourages honest dialogue. If you have created a learning environment (Element 6—**Lifetime Learning**), you team will be less threatened by

probing questions and recognize that you are only seeking an answer and not looking for an opportunity to place blame. The focus is resolving the crisis and not finding someone to blame for it.

6) Take the time to identify the desired outcome— You have to know what you hope to accomplish before deciding on a response. In fact, it is advisable to identify three desired outcomes, encompassing the three most important needs of your team or company (i.e., safety of employees, impact on the environment, health of your business, etc.). This provides the benefit of having a positive outcome to focus the efforts of your team and helps them to learn not to be reactionary.

7) Formulate your action plan and check up periodically on progress of your plan.

You probably won't get this right the first time, but don't be discouraged. Recognize where you have an opportunity to improve and focus on getting it right the next time. More importantly, share your self-evaluation with your team and ask for their input. Once they see you holding yourself to the same standard of learning prevention instead of placing blame, they will be more willing to accept your leadership.

This lesson could very well be a subset of the lesson on **Make it Happen** in Element 5. However, its importance is such that I felt it was necessary to address as a separate element.

Conclusion
The Next Step

Congratulations for reading this series of elements! And, thank you for your interest and for allowing me to share my discovery journey.

Your reaction at this point will take one of several directions:

1) If you have read this work and found no new information, then thank you for simply taking the time. Hopefully, this has reinforced your previous understanding of leadership.

2) If you found only one or two ideas to help you, then your time was not wasted and I hope you continue your personal journey into understanding leadership. This is completely consistent with the advice given in Element 6—**Practice Lifetime Learning**. I encourage you to continue to glean at least one idea from each book you read.

3) For those of you who find wisdom in this book, you may have a tendency to want to make wholesale

changes in your approach to leadership based on these 13 elements. This chapter is mainly written to guide you to a measured course of action that will enhance your probability of success.

Ben Franklin identified 13 virtues which he aspired to master and incorporate into his life. Realizing the difficulty of doing all at once, he arranged them in a logical order so he could begin with one (Temperance) and move to the next as soon as he felt he had mastered each one. The order of his virtues was arranged so that those that impacted later virtues were placed earlier to facilitate the success of learning later virtues. Then, he dedicated a week to each virtue and kept a notebook of his shortcomings so he could see where he needed to improve, with the aspiration that at the end of three months he would see a clean journal with no faults.[24] My selection of 13 elements was not based on Ben Franklin's model. However, it does mesh nicely with his approach.

With this in mind, I offer the three following suggestions:

1) Take adequate time to understand and build your personal vision before starting any other efforts. This may take some time, but it is imperative that you know where you want to take your organization before trying to lead them.

2) Focus on one leadership element for a week at a time before attempting to master the next one. And, consistent with Ben Franklin's method, you

should make diary entries at the end of each day about your successes and shortcomings to heighten your sensitivity to the nuances of each quality. This will substantially enhance your probability for success, since you will not be overwhelmed by the magnitude of the effort and you will be taking the time to understand how each quality affects your leadership ability. Remember success is a journey and not an end. The importance is not in achieving instant mastery of all leadership qualities; it is in constant striving to master them over time. After three months of focusing on each of the elements one week at a time, you should repeat the process. Soon, you will yourself unconsciously correcting missteps in other areas even though they are not your area of focus for the week.

3) Keep your journey to yourself. Resist the temptation to tell your team members or co-workers or supervisor that you are beginning a journey. They will either be looking for examples to show that you are not serious or will look for opportunities to tell you how you have failed. Remember my comment in Element 2—**Effective Communication**, "it is a quirk of human nature that any action or decision will be interpreted as violating your vision unless you are in the field actively communicating the link to people." The same principle applies here. At this point in your journey, just get started. If you are successful, your team members and co-workers (and

probably your supervisor) will notice the change and ask you what you have done differently. That is the time that they will be most accepting and will provide you with the support you need because they have observed a difference in your leadership style. This will also provide you an opportunity to exercise your passion as you tell them of small successes.

I only hope that as you begin your journey into better leadership that you find it as satisfying as it was for me. Thanks again for your time and interest.

References

1   http://archives.cnn.com/2001/TECH/space/05/25/
     kennedy.moon

2   Ibid.

3   Jim Collins, *Good to Great* (New York: Harper Collins
     Publishers, 2001), pp. 197-204.

4   Steven Covey, *The 7 Habits of Highly Effective People*
     (New York:Fireside, 1989) pp. 235-260.

5   T. J. Larkin and Sandar Larkin, *Communicating Change*
     (New York: McGraw Hill, Inc., 1994), p. 94.

6   http://www.businessweek.com/1998/23/b3581001.htm

7   Op. cit.

8   Harvey Pennick, *Harvey Pennicks's Little Red Book* (New
     York: Simon & Schuster, 1992), pp. 12-13.

9   http://www.history.navy.mil/colloquia//cch4c.htm

10   Philip Hodgson & Randall P. White, *Relax, it's only
     uncertainty* (Great Britain: Prentice Hall, 2001), p. 3.

11   Ibid., p.3.

12   Lawrence Miller, *Barbarians to Beaurocrats* (New York:
     Clarkson N. Potter, Inc., 1989), pp. 148.

13   http://hyperhistory.com

14   Lawrence Miller, *Barbarians to Beaurocrats* (New York:
     Clarkson N. Potter, Inc., 1989), pp. 34-58.

[15] Op. cit., pp. 90-119.

[16] Eliyahu M. Goldratt & Jeff Cox, *The Goal* (Croton-on-Hudson: North River Press, Inc., 1984).

[17] Op. cit., p. 160.

[18] Richard Tanner Pascale, *Managing on the Edge* (New York: Touchstone, 1990).

[19] Stephen Coonts, *Under Seige* (New York: Pocket Books, 1991)

[20] Swindoll, *Hand Me Another Brick* (Thomas Nelson, 1978), pp. 82-83; and *Bits and Pieces* (November 1989, p. 12.

[21] Op Cit.

[22] http://leadertoleader.org/leaderbooks/L2L/spring97/kelleher.html

[23] http://www.encyclopedia.com/doc/1G1-55427052.html

[24] http://www.ftrain.com/franklin_improving_self.html